AF522004

Moira of Edges,
Moira the Tart

Moira of Edges, Moira the Tart

Artwork by Moina Pam Dick

Design by Rachael Guynn Wilson & Moina Pam Dick

Text is set in Lusitana and Hind,
with italics in Sabon and PT Sans

ISBN 978-0-578-54455-7

Printed in the United States.
First printing.

This publication is supported in part by
New York University's Department of English.

Available through Small Press Distribution:
www.spdbooks.org

Special thanks to Black Sun Lit
for hosting the OPR as an imprint on SPD.

Organism for Poetic Research
organismforpoeticresearch.org
Brooklyn, New York

Moira of Edges, Moira the Tart

Moina Pam Dick

it's not the new, it is what is yet not known,
thought, seen, touched but really what is not.
and that is.

Eva Hesse
(Exhibition statement: *Contingent*)

...She fall prone.
Only wind whistled.
And forty-seven years went by like Einstein.

John Berryman
(Dream Song 47: *April Fool's Day,*
or, St. Mary of Egypt)

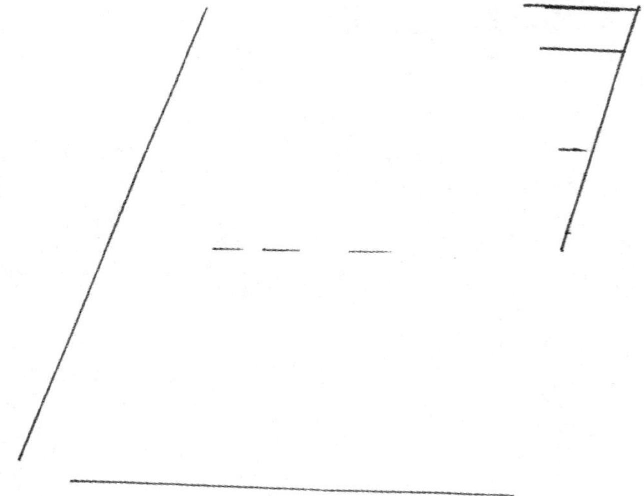

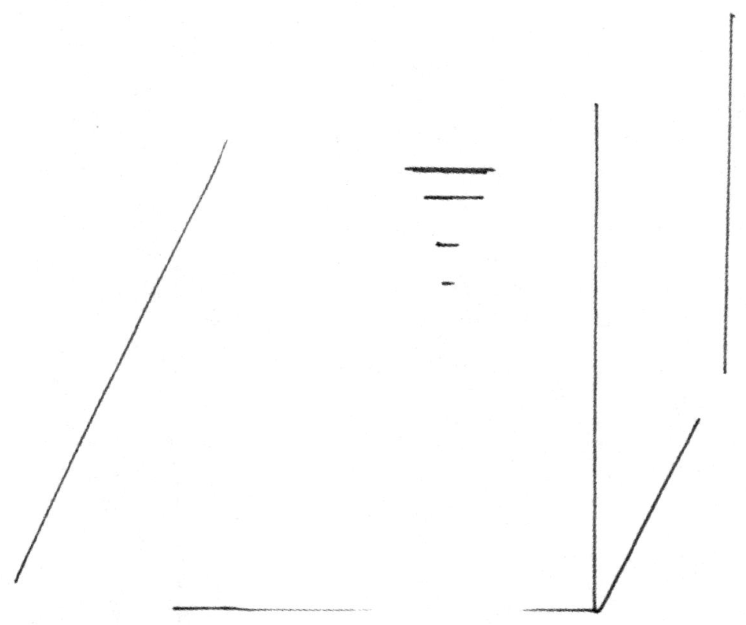

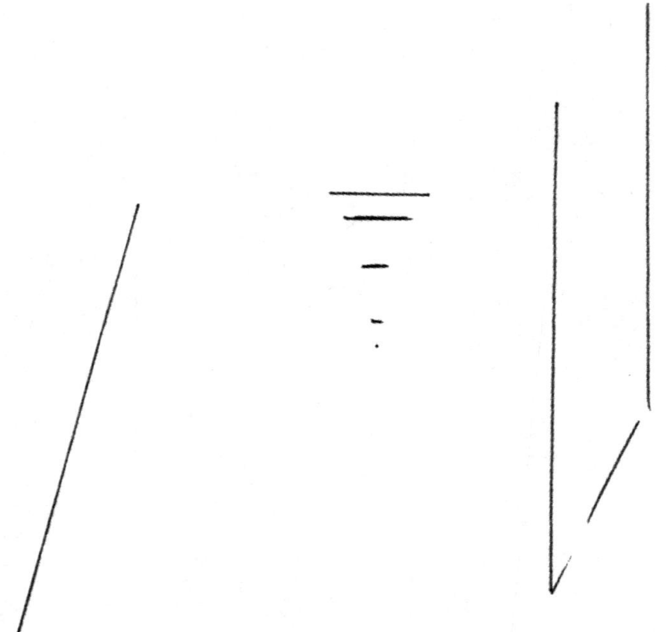

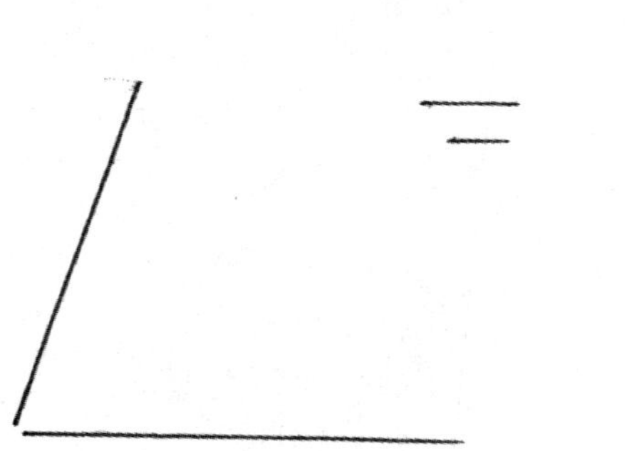

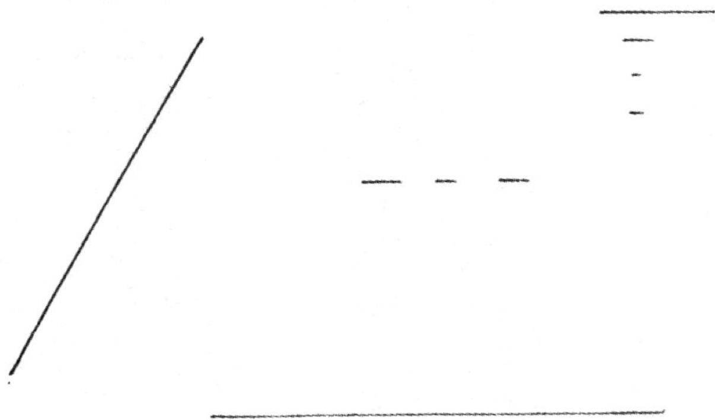

Too much light or not enough?

The sky's translucent whiteness

Or layered, colored planes backlit

Or puns undone

But no! Moholy
Mo' holy
M.o. holy

This is harlot

Right next to blemish point

Pressure, blessure

Polypunctual: rubs all over

Times

Translating down or to flow
Down like her: descender

There was once a certain girl assertion

Moira

Uncertain Moira lived the lines
Lifted hermit

No

Listen, Johnny Mensch

I feel so naked now, will you clothe me?

Your black jacket with the blue,
Yellow, pink, ochre and white
Threads, trims, markings
Your midnight blue cloth or
Ultramarine dark

Your cloak of dreaming

S'ain't Johnny Mensch (first 'man)

And can you bring my hole communion
Next time you come

Paperback
Arid blotter
Lucid wafer

Like Jean Deblanc with his
Whiteness

There was once uncertain color
Of this, my Book of Hours
Errors
Errings
Ors
Whorings
Les heures

Not László's higher

Oh, why not?
There is no
Reason

Does unreason you must eat less

While insatiable

,

Division of a

Marked

Ochre

Punct or

Wait

Way, weigh

She: errant

At th e

Edge

Of

Of

Colored plane

Co lored

Piece cut off

To do or be?

To differ,   wandered

From what died

To beg is no

Is not to

So did not

Still taste his whiteness

Sa blancheur

Black: point or comma

Waiting, wending

Craving shape

,

Was to rubbed

They chose age twelve

She ran, she squandered

"*of insatia—*

She able

Irre press

Able

To refuse

Insist

Re fuse

Ins ist

Tongues Jean

Des heures

De sire

Ran away: the girl of Egypt

To deflower of man

(Alexandria)

Sexually favored

Supple, meant

You spin me 'round

Spinning fucks

Un wordling swervish

Fast in words

With all the

Boys to men

And rubbed

Out seventeen to

Twenty-nine when

(her B series?)

Booked sucked passage

(fondling, say, Brad Davis qua Querelle)

To the feasting Holy City

Sight of

Ex alt—

A sham?

A pill? (To cure her shame less?)
Ill, grin with mortal flash

Or some recursive

Friction's

Epistemic nymph that names this

Tart or tang

And angled toward more pilgrims

Honey, sweet

Spinning flux   flaxen
                              Hair
          Worlding girlish
Versus   silver   vixen

Crazy like a   minx,   clever like an
                    Else

Once they pricked her
          Fingers   balled   hands   fists
          But then   cindered   real of   ashen strumpet

Once when death was playing fluffer

                    Famished, breastless

Starved from   company,   to keep   this

          Moira left with three loaves   staves   to
Lief as   leaving   living

          Took three leaves of
          With me, johns:
          Jean, Johnny, John

Aloft on Daives and Berrymans and Baptizers
                              Not to run out
                    Of leavings
                    Of nevers
                    Of fever's arrows

My clothes are sh   reds,   Moira Jones observes

          So I shelter in my hair, repulse all
          Unruled Rapunzel, godly Rätsel

                              How a line's a curve

,

I was twelve and in geometry
Where is the shape now?

How the desert is a maze and
Time can be a tangle

Or this wild hair hangs in the eyes
So cannot read things but clairvoyant

Still touch and smell inhale the pages—

No, I *can* still read:
"au comme ce ment
f qua re fois

is nter m on sex
pour viv red n cristal"

Is what that Jean's légende laid on my
Tongue so it dissolving

Four times or faiths went cold

Or (not ice) crystals: (sand of desert)
Yellow crystals
Ochre crystals
Grain in eye
Speck on tongue
No ocean's salt

There was one time a certain Moira: divinely struck, destroyed, left
Unconstructed, hearing voices, voix, if vague, or of the void, a null
Les cris tal
L'écrit tell

But was commanded to turn clear

Where is the all?

,
It was   it   not let in

To feast   exalt the hunger

Well-hung girl
Well-formed formula
The dissolute

To try to enter
The
Her   him

The hole   church

Sub ochre (for a sepulchre)

The new sable
Tomb's fable
Le point, la virgule

Sa propre faiblesse   refused, repulsed

Re   pulsed   her
Or what insisted

Invisible force   field   Feld   (second 'man)

To realize *is* doing

The girl paled at how she'd blanched,   skin flecked with impurities

A comma   can strike one with remorse

Lust sex thought orgy: quit this   or   G as   tic
Her day of holy   fool

Look at icon

Blessèd virgin God-baring geometrix Dei

László's yellow, grey, white layers but clear translucencies

Or announced to girlhood Moira, then speed reading sci-fi futurists
(not like László) or Agatha Christ. mysteries (not like Plotinus), or
Søren, Plato, Albert, Jean-Paul, André, Dietrich, Hermann, Fyodor

Or please quit reading? She could not read language, but divinely
Constructed (with ruler, compass, pen, blankness (blanc, vierge) (of
paper)

Discontinue sexed life

For resurrection (see László's child hood or a holy
fool's cap dunce not dense or dense not
sharp unthinking cap purer place)

Bared by a visible

F or ce

Of what dis miss ed

Distance once

Upon a

Time as the form

Crux of paradox of figure
Cross

Raising her eyes' I to

Outside
Outside

Prayed for forgiveness

Promised to re link wish world

I.e. become ascetic aesthetic

at God's image

Then again tried to enter the
Mathesis of
(visual/formal) logic
A line's 0, not
A Lenz ho, a
Church (private), not a profession (public, oldest)

And was
Let her in stripped of her Johns her revolting
Do not self

And after viewing Barnett's recap (abstract, not relic or schematic)
New (third 'man) of the t rue of the Cross
(it was picturate, paint, vocative)
(it is time. The desolate paradox)
(I was once upon four times)
Went back, heard (László's) voice say

Not the other iron voice
(ironic maiden) nor their hate of
Nymphet slut but I's clair voyage

If you cross
The flowing down of Jordan

River, see it from the other side (like Heraclitus)
Find
Glorious

Rest by changing
Verging

So Moira went instanter to (monastic) John Baptizer
He wore hair
Of another God that bit him
Animal
(I just saw him, his story, in a city of wind)

Along the bank of river

(my flowing bangs and long looks when I'm named Moira)

To receive the resolute paradox
The absolute shun

The Wholly Communion

To put his disk in her mouth: bodily symbol, to
Dissolve

This

Then the next dawn (B-series: block, built, before-and-after)

Crossed
My diagram of time?

The new river

(how flow is to improvise)

Retired to
Girly retirement

Immature hermitry

To live
To live as
To live as a pen
I tent

(I transient)

,

To be very clear, naked:
Je tente

Penitent , I try
Tainted, a t tempt
Intent, insist
Transpose lust to
Dis traction to
Abstraction

A holy verging is barely
Touching

At rough edges
If on edge or with God's edge on

(Black sheep, prodigal son, lost girl: desire's potency, divinity)

To rub all over words (punning as word sex, incestuous or homo
phonic syno nymic homo nymph
make nth contact)

But to want the word less

Plain plane
Of drawing's
Touch

But thought's fever still burns me , Moina

(Heraclitus, Plotinus, Benedict, Gottfried, Søren, Arthur)

Could I draw be drawn through, across

The way beyond find rest beat silence

That is
Still, that is
Life?

Moira of Edges loved the ' ones
With
Fevers, lusts, skin diseases, whorings and voracious readings

She bought, i.e. believed
In three scorings

Of moorish Morton
Felt man

(*For Bunita Marcus, Turfan Fragments, Patterns in a Chromatic Field*)

Her clothes tattered, but her longing hair (skirt) not a
Figment leaf staff

Take this
Zero-place predicate
Or
Location sans dimension?

One dimension all?

Now untie the knot of reason to release un-
Reason
To dissolve
The paradox
Of time; the dissolute paradox

It was, was not

Be bare now

If to white circular table, then metaphysics of the cone, to spiral

Down, or faint with gloom, with hunger

But instead, this clings to black ledge, edge, to side
To margin

Not to recognize cognize
Oneself as human
Be metahuman

Barely
Forest
Wasteland, desert

Can I stop now?

Can I stop this now, the now?

Once this was four times, one timeless:

The Arrow (flowing, asymmetric)
The Block (structured, fixed)
The Consciousness (layered, ranging)
The Edge (angled, wanting)
The Dot (dimensionless, full)

This is timepoint—like spacetime, but divided, discontinuous
Yet contiguous: a disparate whole

Four dimensions
Once spacetime had four dimensions,
Three of space and one of time
(now they say others, minute, curling)
Now timepoint has five dimensions,
Four of time and one of timeless
(and dimensionless; how paradox)

Thus point is not reducible to time (in timepoint)
As time is not reducible to space (in spacetime)

(unless Gödel: time is space if relative
and isn't built, block time spatial from outside it? All
the instants simultaneous?)

But Moina, don't do Kurt now!
Curt, girdled, be a cut girl. Edit

But time as space in her belovèd Sienese paintings—

Wait, Moina, stick to thinking!

The edge is not wholly timeless

Is a stillness (anti-time if time is flowing)
Is undated (anti-time if time is fixed, sequential)
Is transcendent (anti-time if time is self's consciousness)

But is *another* time:

Vibration, yearning

Beyond mere rest—mere rest is transient silence
(negative time like negative space between things, as in music)
Beneath pure rest—pure rest is godly stillness
(negative, timeless, the ineffable beyond this)

Whereas glorious rest, shining rest, is when here, arrested, trembling

God arrests you   is the edge time

Where edge is from both
Point (Greek, Latin) and
Corner (German)—
Girlish wedge

This edge as limit of horizontal (terrestrial) plane and vertical (spiritual) plane

And the vertical line of consciousness can move to the edge (with urgent yearning), and then shrink to a point (the pressing)

The instant origin
But this one to One almost never

First must freeze the lower now in focused contemplation

(László) Moholy-Nagy
(Nasreen) Mohamedi
(Agnes) Martin
(Piet) Mondrian
(Kazimir) Malevich

Is what (Jones) Moira

Could not read but divinely inspected

Lived on lines and colors
Shapes, composings

Luminous geometries
(not geometric method)

Is the desert plane

Or what inscribes there

In sharpness

Keen of argument
Of form
Of want desire

Pictorial language
Philosophical of
Brink or verge
Or of an image

Ice rink, girl edges
Skates on thinner ice
Is as walks on water

Nervous, acutely sensitive

Impatient is not now

In desert, waiting

If I could be Moira
Barely human

Écoute-moi, Johnny Mensch

It was two: red to pink, near to smaller

Scarlet filter (grade school stagelight, strumpet's
halo (hooky with a head of gold), stay gold,
Punyboygirl)

And to cut by the yellow, back to black and as crosses

Where shapes touch, overlap, the color changes, as translucent

Two were floating as the moments
Or the versions

Like two Johns: two Baptizers, when he as youth
Leaves to be a saint
And time is passing

The simultaneity of moments is a built series: left to right (one fixed
image)

The female saint who was three times (size gradations)

One time walks across a river

Her ochre landscape is humility, while *her* humiliation church
Refused her

Or two Jeans (le français et/and English)
Doubled pages, senses, shapes

Representational or abstract
Light brown of sand, support of surface

If two floating
This way absent from the grid of checkerboard
Of order, system to a wave form
As a wilderness

Sci-fi abstraction or Nasreen: her shapes as moments

Time turns to space

Or remember: Moira drew the saint, the light bulb shape, three times
(premonition of departing thrice: Manhattan, Alexandria, Jerusalem)

Thus imagine her thin cone shape as she's
Leaving

Three's recursion (St. Umiltà/Humility in the painting
from with in John Evangelizer)

Or rectangular as strip of brown or yellow
Grey or silver or a cluster of fine lines
Of threads or flax as verticals

Therefore 14th century or Modernist because abstract
(the Sienese of shape and composition)

2D/3D frisson of vibration

Now do Lazarus (as if László) raised or risen

Did I die last night,
Did Moira die no
Jonesing?

Moina Jones of Moira Jones of insatiable: dissatisfaction sequence

But when deadened, then no series

Moira frenzied, Moina palsied
Do not show that

How tones change when shapes layer, interacting
Joy of edges

Is construction or destruction
Or constructed to destroy oneself
Built to pass, be less
The lass to fast
The loss to fist

So Moira of Edges, translucent

Brightness beyond edges

Leaving the convenient of convention, goes to
Wildness

(is this covenant?)

Almost unrecognizable as artwork or as human

Don't think; seek
Don't balk, stroke
So feels, intuits:

Wholes, holes, parts, particles, points, voids, edges, shapes

They say a God -shaped ho

Or void, divine
Her divination
Of the distant

Johnny, will you bring
Not come
But union

If I tell you still more of my life time?

Here, take your cloak back

And see through me, I am ghostly

Feeling night of hollow (in be) tween

,

If too long and

If too long

And thick et
Et le fourré

Of not yet lightness

His white circle or *his* yellow

Be with dead ones

What unfinished incompleteness

Cave or closet

If skin tan or too pale, blue

The translucence

Or the skin on heated milk (see bed
time)

Or the coat of white wall paint

Or the harder cloud of glue

But not glued to this seen

How time is moving

Which is

Moves this?

While her girlish

Truth (called *The Mortal*)

Dies prematurely?

It was Dante (yes, she pinched him, sampled, rubbed his contours)

It was cone as in a

Spiral
Thought's

Purgation

First girl of 12 acting 21, then of 29 looking 20, then of X looking 29
(for decades missing), then of 47 (Johnny's dream song) looking '77
From unkempt silver hair and scrawny form/figure? Or does Moira
Still look youth?

Cf. Nasreen's age when she

Long-haired virgin girlish

Hide behind or

Veil her edges

Now transparent

Now too hot

Too cold

But was to re think time

And why no conversion yet, for this?

Why is this struggle not yet past?

,

Which is still, which moves?

The two series: one independent, the other relative

Thus directions?

Imagine two trains halted in a station
Inverse directions
Then you don't know which
Commences moving

Outside the now (of the A series), all the moments exist equally
In the built, the block of the B series

You could be any   where if the   now would

Release you   (cf. Gödel's time travel)

It grew light too quickly, I missed dawn, the transition

The illogic that you are still, time flows by you from the future to the
Past (in the string of dated moments)

When in fact, the sequence is unmoving, you are rushing forward

The feeling of stillness, because the consciousness is always in the
Now

But no, consciousness can roam, inhabit other instants, make those
Its now or knot them into the now

So there are two nows, the objective and the subjective?

Or separate the now from consciousness?

The flow of time is series A. It has you in its current, moves forward,
Keeps arriving at new instants

The block of time is series B, the river's bank, moments fleeting,
Flashing by

Two ways of stopping time:

1) to leave the present, now, observe all times as equal

2) to love the present, now, shun other times as gone, unreal

To cleave or to cleave to?

Detachment or attachment?

Either way to spirit

Severs contact of two series subtracts friction

Stop your rubbing, Moina

But it's *consciousness* that does this:

Shifts, veers off, detaches

The subjective as the textured

Mind as tangled or as layering?

Indexical (demonstrative)
Structural (objective)
Textural (subjective)
Marginal (subtractive)
Punctual (contractive)

She could conjure several moments and be in them at a single now or
In those paintings

Even if with different scales or tone or just positions

Therefore the mind, when it is light, transmutes the body

So the matter becomes energy

And instantaneous, as speed of light
(as C for consciousness)

Jean Deblanc says one of the tones is declared C

The shade of ochre, light blue, yellow?

Now the hour/time effaces his *mortal fable*
My *mortal truth*

Wanting to call to C your consciousness?

Or (she'd say) Christ or a John Chrysostom? Climacus?

Always more of her johns (four at a time one time)
But do not touch them

But to shrink from the textural, complex to edge, then point

Contracting, lose dimension
I long to do that, I
Cannot do that
The most to hope for is translucency

By new transparency
My frank confession
But refracted

Or to focal point

Or reach the fucking point

Contract to God spot

Break

So her lust
It is non-narrative
It is at once
It is in instants
It is dispersed
It is repeats

Comme/as   promis   cuous

Not cash
But rush

Is it compulsive   is disorder?

Please don't enter   art's frottage
(or am I queer man   girl
shorn like a male)
As of Moira: edge, not wedge
Permits rear entry

When the tart was just a girl, gave chocolate valentines to Aleks,
Juan, Sami (city of Alexandria, Book of John/s, verse of Rumi)

((Church of Jerusalem))
It was the small, quick, blond, remote one
Funny, slight, charming and
Will never   x   him

Ribs or hips, wrists or clothèd cocks

I can't help it if the one point's all that
Is   ungirlish

But, too, not sensual. How bodies per se swiftly bore this

It's the spirit   or   emotion   charge   the   mental

And the rub on

Sparks the god off

Therefore askesis is the natural

As the asking

And to longing

But to sacrifice the thoughts

The signs of logic
Or geometry or algebra

Or Russian, Spanish, French

But that place

The voice

Conversion is

The comma

So to *strike*

Or chop the phrase

How to keep going?

There were two, as Augustine or Dante

Once two Moiras

Or else four were fois

Once four times

Four different faiths?

What happens at the end is after ,

Speaks, tells all, to perish

Does that night, but magically
Unchanged and is trans ported 'lated

Meta

To be found alongside flow (when time was river)

Johnny, meet me

Then a lion boy (not Ponyboy) like Jalal of Rûm (cf. László of Mohol, called by place of childhood) helps to bury

(Johnny, bury me you are my first 'man among men)

Or like preteen Aslan?

His warm breath

Ponder breath
Strike her end?
Bring back comma?
The second comma of Moira Jones?

After which, I can be Moina?
Moina Jones?

To stretch out
Let this flow
Follow curves

Clinch the edge

How many times can one convert?

Be called to

Green

Periphery, epiphany

When new
It would not let me in

The thought as dwelling

This green notebook

Iteration's irritation
Skin

Rhymed scheme

Him

To fall in love with

With Jalal means glorious

It rests by
Urging, ranging

Variable, over

Con version

Re cursion
Lion

Lines converging

Intersection of two lines is a point

Taste burning

C'est l'urgence
Of yearning

From point in time to point detached:

The antidot

La virgule blanche?

Negation

Where shift of

In location

Time to

One

In the beginning One created

When was
Breath less

Once I commenced four times
J'ai été foudroyée at once

Then I de terred my

Sex in cave

To live

(cast/spun off)

Not distaff

Distal

Moira found her peace?

It rests by edging

Moina falls for verse?

Jalal room or rim me

Voice charging

To this going

Rests by dervish

To start *again*, I had to touch this

Rip or staining

Deep immersion

No form

Moving

Opens window, noise invades

Breath revives

Spins, condensing

Bird and blue

Panting pants

Hairless shirts

Restless panties

(green, white, violet)

Or hung, dangled

Downward

Up

Way to One

Form and matted

Skip (the) rope
Striking chord

Replace

Meant theorem with
with

Delirium
Calling

Not Johnny Mensch, but Eva Heiße

She and Moina ride Jamal of Reams (divinely tawny lion)

Take him to the limit

With the edgy neon glow strokes

To a laughter

,

Motion's stillness

Helix, vortex

Then contracting

A city truck said *edge*, and it was whiteness

While I walked toward the East River (all was sign, was signage)

Arrow as index (three tensed parts, moving series)
Block as symbol (all date points, fixed series)
Chord as icon (consciousness, moving set)
Edge as inverse (desire, vibrating set)
Point as locus (one element, fixed nought)

They wrote that time is the moving image of eternity

I said that *edge* is the vibrating image of eternity

Until it condenses

My vertical, height's horizontal
To one full nil

(punctuate paradox)

In location @no

Where

(whole,
not
pixel)

,

If to

Gyrate

Of

Inverted

Thus the cone as spiral

Not time's or spirit's form, but *to be, to do* it

(extend the arms and spin, a conic dervish—or keep arms down, be angled line, inscribe a whirling cone in air)

Draws God down, inward

Draws one down, inward

To

One's self

Not penitent, nor waiting

Rather, what if Moira drew

On fallen leaves, on bark

With dirt and berries?

,

It to dusk

Lit rooms or planes

This twilight construct

Wild plane meets world plane at edge (the vertical meets horizontal)

While the *other* horizontal (God plane) floats above

Quit mind and now, their wandering

With

Twirling girlish

Not to bury her

Like Him

When Johnny Mensch fell into

(did not cross, walk upon)

The river

Sucked into flow

Interred his x

(word berry-stained)

Forgot the

Glory of the lion

,

Wrests by virgin

Persian covering

Radiance

Or naked, honest

Franche

Blancheur

Tawny

Ochre

Yellow

Now's rain green

Or Eva's golden

Fabric, model, shred

I saw her

Test

Piece for

Contingent

,

Not

But beauty crossed

Sublimity

It wrists by gyrate

If possession's self to lose the mono in humility

Young men hold hands, about to venture to a God place

She as Moira says give body
To ideas, flirts with manhood, curveless
(chest as light
swatch)

If men fight (her callousness untruth) or strange knights halt her

Then blissèd other of God, verging
Spin of
Heaven
László's picture or *all* form is rebellion?

Thrusts by hinging God sum of

To trust to plainness?

Thought stains planes not

Flight or light

Divine topology

Fights graphic

Theory

The plane of built time (sempiternal block, temporal parts), the
Horizontal vector of now's flow time (fleet present), the vertical
Chord of mind's time (extended, impure present), the vertical line of
Edge time (intensified, pure present), the contraction to a point (pure
Eternity)

The metaphysical structure: World (matter/meaning)
Soul (force)
Mind (consciousness)
Spirit (love)
One (null/source) (Cf. Plotinus)

The block fixing all in place permanently, a sign that is convention,
Symbol, quasi-spatial sequence

The arrow dividing time into (shifting) past, present, future as it
Moves, emitted from One's eternity, its moving effect, index

The mind's chord twisting together plural moments as it moves yet
Sustains; eternity's iterating image, its formal likeness, icon

The edge of spirit's line when mind has thinned and fled to margin,
Turns inward, rotates focus upward; eternity's vibrating image,
Insufficiency, want, inverse

At first this line is passive, yearning, vibrating, waiting for God.
Then it realizes it must act to bring God to it. So it spins, becomes
Conic generator, cone's edge, whirling spiral. Vortex. (Cf. Rumi.)
Reversing the order, relationship between God and Spirit. Inverting
It. Like walking on your head. So that it might shrink to a point

I would like to suck in my God.

(cf. Büchner's Lenz)

First, it slid to side of world
(untethered from a Now of immanence)

Then it vibrated
(gathered in a Now of imminence)

Then it spun

Sucks God plane, crumpled, into it

And itself: swallows itself

Or how a sheet of paper burns, curls

It evaporates

The role of burning

Heraclitus' fire

Volatility

@the edge, where two planes touch
(planes of world and ardor)

And the third, the God plane (air)

Folding in, like fevered origami

Or crushed to point

(from goal to inward)

In God's fist that is your twisting

To gather cyclone

Outside in
Other fisting

To reach point

G-spot is God locus

Of dimensionless location

Of unfixed/fixed position

Of the heaven, kingdom

Here, below

Is above

The ways up and down the same

The place up and down

Is here and there and

Nowhere

Position immeasurable

When God's momentum

In the point, there is still motion?

To make fast?

The imperative of paradox

Xenomotion

But wait: time's arrow, line is not straight? It veers mazelike,
Curving. Or is cyclical. Or repeats itself—its character?

How to depict the strange objective closeness of distant moments,
The doubling back and repetitions, variations?

Three possible forms: Tangle
Helix
Repeated notes (motifs/phrases)

Isn't it the latter? Thus still use plane and vector, but the block's
Horizontal strips bear colors (tones). Some separated strips are close
In color. No repetition is exact. And the mind remains a chord.
Though also node (so Eva's tangles). Some lines of your past (your
future?) knotting into the present—

Is a chord a knot—
A fused, folded-inward string segment?

But the world plane as historical must be doubled by another plane,
Your plane, as individual, personal. (Particularity of presentation.)
This can't be captured by the vertical chord, stack of consciousness

Then the chord of mind tethers the world plane, its Now, to your
Plane and Now?

Or is the block of time, its wide plane, already personalized—either
Your time as *part* of world time, a much vaster plane, divided into
Individual rectangles/strips/regions, or your time as hovering above
World time, one of its parallels, echoes?

If the former, colored rectangles lie adjacent. If the latter, they sit
Layered

Either way, László, Eva

Halt this, Moina! Clear away, restart; breathe deep, let thoughts float
In (throw off disproof, its spent rules, for poem/pamphlet: leaves in
quire)

,

Heat of breath

God plane's air

Vapor marks the Spirit

This *other* incarnation
Girl's incarnation:

Fire, electricity

(not haunted mind, but wanting)

Living, moving on the edge

Height, depth

Yet wind
To air
To skyward

Speech (in tongues) balloon

Was flux- or flexwork

Criss-crossed lines
Rhymed skeins

Clothed
In sky, I saw it

,

To be God's

Edge then point

This abstract marginalia

Become source senseless force

Thus to focus

Shed two series

(A), (B)

Shrink the set

(C)

Be edge, pure ardor, yearning

(E)

Until null (de-, devoid)

(D)

(transliterate *abyssed*)

What is the wind?

Is it produced by currents?

Or it skims them?

If to think on/of water

Cross the river to you

Johnny

Not to enter

So my feet

Remain unclean?

But

Inspiration

Inhalation

Tongues are flaming

Exhalation

Emanation

Hot breath touches scorches

To transfigure body

Into

Edge and

Rush of glowing

Vapor, plane as energetic

Now to shape it

How Moholy-Nagy would depict it

Colored planes in layers with lines with geometric figures

Is clear and luminous, but is not simple

Is pure yet complex, is vertiginous

Is paradox

The Distillate Paradox

If only this could concentrate harder, compress words' dissonance

Or clumsy, leaning, dangling forms

To render bliss

This clouded

This vaporous

By successive

Evaporation

Dissolving into thinness

Or condensation

Denser

Lay out flat

Or crush to

Gleaming point

To *philosophize* like

Eva
Jalal
László

(or like Morton)

To be liquid

Not as gush
(high proof, effusive, lush)

But drops

Small yet incessant, insis tent

To quench

To impart in small

To exude minute

To be wet with or

To

Fraction

Moina@ Edge

To

Purify by successive

Essence

Volatility

Evaporating or vaporizing reading/readily

Do you want to vaporize or liquefy?

Again the thoughts erratic
Whor ling

Touching, whoring

Hypersensitive skin

Blue

Skein of veins or nerves

Or tap to pierce this

But now *draw*

Draw God down

Not

Death

(her) death

Inscribed in sand
Its instant
(name)

(or smash the hourglass, then walk on it)

Floor plane transposed

To edge's

Sharpness
Clarity

De   sired

Sear

To   w   ill   to wait
(in   tense)

Past time

As lust

Pure eye dis   tills it

Not to qui   et   but to

Burn with joy

Turning, spinning
(not Søren's top,
nor Johnny's toy)

Thus redirect

Condense

To point

As Moira

As

Of Gyrates

(gyres)

To marvel
@ (discern)

Divine ’ wild feel

If clothèd

Edge

Sand died a way

Her said?

Her narrative?

Turn of page

To spiral off to

What could hap pen after?

Not when return to thick of world (left, back)

But when advance to full of whirl (right, forward)

Page of plane: new color, glow divine translation

With edges (gutter, outer) still to move to, from:

Recursion, transience

But this new immanence

Form of the book

Past ever-marginal

Transabstraction of the world

Relit to recto

Glows like

Eva's yellow sheets

László's yellow shapes

Moina's yellow stretches

(Moina of Verges, Moina of Pages)

Whirling girlish

Conic method

Dash to color

Felt tip moves

Bright-Out, High, Lighter!

Liquid's

Paper

Dissolves

Re solves

Is salve

To stain with God blot

Write the drawing

Fast when still

Clear

Yet

Blur

If God tops you

Is this vortext?

Acknowledgments

Appreciation to all the writers, artists and thinkers with whom this text dallies.

An excerpt from an earlier version of this work appeared in *PELT v. 4, Feminist Temporalities*, published by OPR in 2017; my thanks to the editors.

Deep gratitude to my publisher/editor/co-designer Rachael Wilson and my first reader-responders Anselm Berrigan and Lucy Ives, as well as to Oana Avasilichioaei, Genya Turovskaya, Brett Price, Sylvia Brownrigg, other friends and family.

This book is for Genya.